The Moon on Elba

The Moon on Elba

POEMS

ANDREW FRISARDI

Wiseblood Books

CONTENTS

For Daphne

The Moon on Elba

1. The Clearing

Often I am permitted to return to a meadow.

—Robert Duncan

WORD

Word is hello, is house,
The arrival in the ride.
It is the root that grows,
The uttered oath, the bride
Beside, before the altar,
Before decisions falter.

Word is the inside-out
Of loneliness's pillow,
The certainty of doubt,
A shimmer on a billow
At the horizon's edge
Beyond the garden hedge.

Word is white before
Its colors can begin
To chronicle its lore.
It speaks our speaking: in
The beginning was the word,
It's what the silence heard.

Word, in time, we break
Or give, spread or keep.
It may ring true when fake,
Taken on faith, asleep.
Adam and Eve would fault
A word for their lost gestalt.

Word is the tongue on watch
For what might crack the crust,
The thumbprint ash, the blotch
On a brow, forecast of dust.
Its breath is what engenders
Breath in the earth it renders.

It is the code of law
That conquers kings with a sword
Too fine for shock and awe.
A spaceship carries word
In a time capsule. Its nib
Is the point of Adam's rib.

THE JEWELER

From poshness up at Sotheby Parke Bernet
To jostles down on Forty-seventh Street,
The Brazilian's workshop is a world apart,
Several stories up an office block
Whose elevators turn to iron cauldrons
When summer weather stews the city in smog.
On the street, in throngs of long black coats, Hasidim
Pass around fat envelopes of diamonds
As casually as if they're sharing lunch.

Above, Haraldo is working at his bench, a loupe
Wedged against his eyeball, plying metals.
In keeping with his Latin looks, his shop
Is charmingly Old Worldy, nonchalant,
The odd appurtenances of his trade
Scattered about the place in easy chaos.
He works the silver, platinum, or gold,
Pouring a pile of brilliants for pavé
Like crumblets sprinkled from a dragon's mouth.
He sets a ruby big as a thumbnail,
Knowing its truest red appears by angling,
Nudging it like fishing line, a lure
Or bait that's cast strategically in water.
He might hold up an emerald in a cleft

Between his fingers near his knuckle bones
And dandle it in daylight by a window,
Its color like a patch of Irish grass,
Or else green fire from Venus an astronaut
Trapped and carried back, its coals intact.
He deftly tweezes it between the prongs
He's wrought. The art's to make it natural,
He thinks: exploit the flaws and angle the light.

Sometimes you'll find Haraldo there with Jain,
A youngish Indian who lives in Queens,
Polite and gentle, often with a bag
Of goodies—star sapphires, black pearls, or garnets
From Russia, the pine-green ones called demantoid
(You tell them by the horsetail shapes inside),
And rubies Jain will claim, rolling his *r*'s,
Are nothing less than "Burmese. Guaranteed."

One August day Haraldo had his smock on,
Sweating like he'd been welding auto parts.
Jain's head was down like someone had just died,
Which someone almost had. In Jain's building
A dealer had been robbed the night before,
His safe left like a junked refrigerator.
"He was the last one open," Jain explained.
"They held him up at gunpoint, bound and gagged him . . .
Young, too . . . with wife and kids . . . you never know."

Jain paused, his face and shirt still neat though drenched
With sweat, his manner steady-as-you-go.
Haraldo, meanwhile, seemed about to snap—
A combination of the news and heat.
"It's asinine what easy hits we are,"
He muttered, glancing at his bench's bunch
Of old-cut diamonds from an antique brooch,
Their idiosyncratic shapes a play
Of polar light sequestered in the ozone.
"I work alone here evenings sometimes too."
He picked a diamond up. "It's just a rock,"
He said, "but it makes people go berserk
To get it. Money talks but jewels sparkle."

THE MOON ON ELBA

The moon is the sun on vacation. Peeping on Elba,
It sauntered and climbed like a vine creeping on Elba.

It's been said that the moon is mad, a disturbance in blood:
Just right for soccer fans and dancers leaping on Elba.

It was, as usual, corrupting the parchments of light,
Or else that night would be in safe keeping, on Elba.

Couples and families strolling the shore looked out
On the waves to admire what the moon was heaping on Elba.

Heartbreak is best in a song, but when it's in life
And unsung, you could do worse than be weeping on Elba.

It makes zero sense! Why are the gods always hungry?
What is the sum of the lives they were reaping on Elba?

I dreamed up a fortune teller and drew a card—
The Moon, of course. And went on sleeping on Elba.

SLUGS

Elastic lengths of bodies graze the greens,
Entirely tongue, information gleaners

From the planet Earth. A berry bomb
The blackbird dropped has sounded an alarm

That shudders yellow in the heart of broom,
But nothing they will do will happen soon.

Gentle antennae probe scientifically
Into beads of water, past amoebae,

All the way to a convex mirror's shore.
Pay attention: A slug's a pioneer

Of time. Such is the start of stars and coal:
It's out of sight or, maybe, not at all.

THE CLEARING

Swallows are playing the air above the field
From highs to lows. Oh wow, they play so fast,
Like wild violinists' bows that meld
Their tempos to the seeded tips of grass.
Like that, and just like that their dips and jerks
Become berserk batons, collectively
Conducting devil-feathered tuning-forks
For Symphony in Z, a fickle key.

The clearing seemed abandoned and subdued,
But as I start across they've improvised it.
And just like that, again like that, they've wed
The composition of the field to sheer
Surprise, as if a movement that infused it
Is boomeranging in the shapes of air.

EARLY RISER

The dark is petaled, fleshy like a lily,
And dew is magnifying a dot of day,

When fingers pivot on an icy grip
To swing a door out from a rockface room,

As motes of thought too inchoate to say
Drift slantwise slowly on a draft of dreams,

While moulting light wheels back from far away
To flutter down like feathers at the arms,

And the creaking man-frame settles in its nook
To find a chair and board and an open book.

THE VIRGIN MARTYR

It wasn't just that she refused to doff
Her honor to a lie so she might live.
What really pissed her persecutors off
Was that her love did nothing positive
For the economy. Why not do what
Her father said? He wanted her to be
A dowry not some flitting spirit's slut.
Instead, her lap and torso formed a *C*
Around the unknown life that entered her
When she was praying all alone one day
Beside a lily. When she felt it stir,
To get it out they burned the *C* away,
But only saw a mote. Nobody knew
It was the seed of charity that grew.

Fall in Five Movements

I. *Dowry*

What did it start with? It was the merest hint,
A crimson pod that banged me on the pate,
Its scraping as it ghost-percussed the pavement.

Only devotion lasts: a reservoir
That fills the space where Ruth clung to Naomi
When they left with poverty, her dowry.

Which remnants of life I recognize will matter?
My weathervanes are swaying underwater.
When the trees have lost their leaves, crows will gutter

On branches. When the night's wool batting tamps
My sight, my empty hands will turn to lamps.

II. *Equinox*

From motionlessness, motions start.
A gust revives the autumn day.
Just look at how the shadows sway
That rustling stalk of leaves, your heart.

III. *Dramatis Personae*

At bedtime I undress-rehearse for death.
And I am getting pretty good at it, too.
Because I'm me, I play myself no sweat,
And self-forgetfulness is impromptu.

IV. *Stars*
(All Souls)

When I look out my window, set to pray
To a distant God, I'm startled by a glow
Like fires of scattered campsites in the sky,
As if my dead are nearer than I know.

V. *The Owl*

I hear the owl on a branch out back,
Screeching the one question I have ever heard
Whose answer is the same come glut or lack.

I want a glimpse of her unflinching vision,
To finally make, before the day's first word,
A single irrevocable decision.

ENVOY

Out for a walk one day
Along a road alone
Heading back toward home
As bright air turned to gray,
It's odd, but I could swear
I saw my body there,
Forming out in front
Like some illusionist stunt,
The air a sprouting seed
Whose shoots were filigreed
In traceries of breath
Draped with bone and flesh
And branching out as me,
A human walking tree
Hoisting his roots, while I
Was keeping pace to try
To catch up with this man
Who had grown alien,
A foil to what I was,
Striding where I strode
In lockstep love because
We walked along the road
Toward our shared abode.

MEDITERRANEAN

The days fly by but the moments traipse.
Sing it, cicada, summer's daemon:
How air is singed till the sun's semen
Incinerates the mother of grapes.

Drifting glints on a brackish splash
Are seeds of coals in the sea's brazier,
As breakers stir the everywhere azure
Into an ecstasy of ash.

II. Purgatorial Portraits

Io riconobbi i miei non falsi errori.

—Dante, *Purgatorio* XV

THE DISTANCE
Castiglione in Teverina, Spring 2020

Covid left us cold in the wake of winter.
Then the numbers, northward, vertiginally
Mounted. Storefronts shut. And the hours unrippled,
Pooled in our closing.

Teverina's trees were a pause in music,
Empty staves of branches that dripped *piano*
Interludes of silence. The Tiber Valley
Harmonized distance.

Painted rainbow *Ce la faremo* banners
Grinned in windows children had decorated.
Neighbors sang together in twilight choirs
Balconies lofted.

Held to household angles, we walked in circles.
Army trucks up north on the television
Solemnly disgorged the remains in churches
Morgues were disguised as.

Casalpusterlengo, Codogno, Lodi,
Lombardia, Bergamo, Terranova,
Castiglione d'Adda, Milano, Brescia:
Names that were falling.

August at the church of the Snowy Mary
We will feign a flurry amid the swelter,
Soapsuds blown out from a machine above us,
Laundering *afa*.

Sailing clouds will dock in the blue of morning:
Back at last in Italy, bliss of exiles,
Shelley said, so many are right at home in
Breaching the distance.

THE SWEEPER

He came to us one day in all his grimness
To purge the hardened tar that crimped our chimney.
He came to us as if a silhouette.
Grumbling greetings, he unlatched his kit
Of grips and metal bits with wire meshes,
And screwed in place the mother of all brushes.
He dragged out from a plastic sack his hide
For inside, harsh with char, and pulled its hood
Up on his head to shinny into darkness.
We hung a sheet to claim the fire's carcass,
Around the flame-devouring mouth of hearth
That spat the felled dismemberings of his art.
He plied his scrubber like a metal mole
Sounding out the measure of his hole.
We were relieved to listen to the bristles
Grate old winter nights' combusted dust,
All that was left of bonds to soothe our sores.
We loved to hear the slough of spent desires.
His mouth still blind to words, the man pulled free
His head from all that past. An unclogged flue
Is a freed soul, he seemed begrudgingly
To grant, and scrunched his brush to pure potential.

An Old Cassette-Letter

One side is you, the other's me, recorded
After I'd moved away when we were young.
At odds, we clung. We couldn't have afforded
To lose each other, we were both so strung
On complementary hurt: my ulcered tongue,
Your guttural self-doubt. These days I'd say
To us: *Let go. Before long we'll be flung*
Beyond the range our voices have today.

But what's the use? I couldn't say it then,
And I've survived, while you, by choice, have not.
Your words, straining as if to free your thought
At last, replay inside my heart again,
In starts and stutters that I wouldn't hear
If what became of distance were not near.

FAMILY SNAPSHOT

for my brother

We're shapes suspended in the tinted grains,
Making faces on our parents' laps.
The four of us are happy: Christmas Eve
On Hawthorne Street. Our troubles mere mishaps,
We're blind to what might be up Fortune's sleeve.
We smile at *cheese,* having no cause to fret
About the night behind us in the panes.

A flash. The years, like light that's fading, lapse.
We're looking into eyes we don't know yet.

FORGIVENESS

i.m. my stepmother

You were a secretary where my dad
Was working. At his office, when we met,
I didn't know your secret love—not yet.
My mother's strength concealed her nights were sad.

You talked to me, the only grownup there
Who did, and smiled as if I were the son
You wished was yours. Your touch and sense of fun
Were warm as colored lights with Christmas near.

You led me to a window to exclaim,
"The snow is magic, isn't it!" On Main,
The feathered tarmac roosted with a brood
Of shoppers hatching into white, renewed.

I wish I could get back that moment now,
With all my childish trust, no matter how
We hated in the end what we became.
Our hearts were light as snowflakes, free of blame.

ASSIMILATION

I. *American Dream*

You waved from Newbury and Berkeley, dressed,
As usual, in a proper business suit
(Your immigrant's wish). At your nod's behest
I tagged along like your far-fetched recruit.
Pedestrians were on the go, fast-forward
To our slow-mo—a foreign film's preview.
Yours might have been about an English lord,
Mine Dante. We forgot our lines on cue.

Along the storefronts of the posh boutiques
You window-shopped for what a Wasp respects
And I despised, admirer of acid freaks,
Rockers, and father-figure intellects.
You were from Rome, well-dressed and dignified,
No Virgil but a merchant as my guide.

II. *Repatriation*

The past I dreamed just now is air. The future
Is here, your mouth forgetting how to say
What once seemed clear, now that the famous moocher,
Time, has sponged your mind up into gray.
I hold you on a treadmill that is still
As a sidewalk. We are all pedestrian
At story's end, though tilting at our mill
Might sometimes make us feel equestrian.

At the therapist's, wearing bone-dry sweats,
You glower when I ask, "Are you alright?"
(Habitual survival tack). Regrets
Won't help your emigration into night.
Pausing to rest before you have begun,
You finally blurt: "*Basta*. Are we done?"

As If Eden Never Happened

Adam and Eve trudge home late from tilling
The fields, splash off some dirt, rub
Together their chapped and aching hands.
Adam pokes the embers in the fire.
Eve offers a tired breast to Cain's
Cantankerous need. Abel isn't born yet;
Already the Original Couple is at a loss.
God never sentenced them to this, never
Cursed them. They can't remember feeling young.
No interval of milk and honey,
No spring-fed stream, no animals
To name. No unashamed nakedness.
What they wouldn't give now for a serpent,
Some blind temptation to ignite their world;
An angel with a flaming sword standing guard
Over the garden they were never evicted from.

SILVER SELVES

Why did we two forsake it,
Senseless or naïve
      About the things we were about to leave?
We used to wander naked
Like loosey-goosey gods
      On our home turf, still favored by the odds,
Our parents still alive,
Our garden walled and native,
      Until our fruit-tree picking got creative,
And east of there we lost
What we forgot. It cost

Us, left us fugitive
For years along a road
      That has no route. By now, our running slowed,
We've settled down to live.
Our open cut is far
      From where our past is sutured in its scar,
A garden with fruit trees
And corner sanctuaries
      Our daily wish is answered by. It queries
Clemency that heals
What binding choice congeals.

If being is a given
Our living makes cohere,
Our origin, though far away, is here.
Our past is with us, hidden.
We've stored away by stealth
Our self-sequestered silver's tarnished wealth
To savor our defeat
Until we're obsolete.
In the meantime, love, we live. We take and eat
Our present-past in fruits
Still pulpy with our roots.

A LITERAL DEATH

When I, as we say, died,
My exit was bone-slow.
I hovered at my bedside
And felt the wind blow.

I felt the wind although
The hospital door was shut.
I didn't want to go.
My fear congealed a cut:

A cut like the tapered crack
Of a door off its jamb.
And now, the air is black,
I don't know where I am.

I don't know if I'm back
At supper with my wife,
Like a hypochondriac
Convinced he's lost his life,

Or in the old back yard,
With my kids raking leaves.
My life was a canard
An unreal dead man grieves.

THE PRISONERS

Michelangelo's unfinished sculptures, the Accademia Gallery, Florence

You, tourist, pondering our jagged girth,
Picture our bodies as they might have stood,
As if our mineral hoods and mantles could
Be shed like chrysalises. Our stuck birth
To you seems like the burden of a beast.
Our maker left us rough, swaddled in stone
Without a saving chisel, each alone
In company and bent to be released
From hindrances we feel but cannot see
Or shatter. Such inflexible husks hurt
And keep our coiled potency inert,
Straining our muscles in the will to be.
Imagining that marble chokes our cries,
You're bound to carve our freedom with your eyes.

An Old Poet

I'm never soberer than when I'm drunk.
My turkey's cold, my blustering is bunk,
And I scare crows. Has the old boy bogged down?
My life's a box of blown-up joke cigars.
I live alone and fill the glass, to drown
In distillations of terrestrial stars.

III. Diptych Nativity

Nothing gold can stay.
—Robert Frost

LATE WINTER DAWN

Let there be light. —Genesis 1:3

Raindrops go still on leaves, letting
Birds rouse in the drenched netting
Of the slow-sap branches. The chink
Of light, the crystal hoop
That is nowhere, opens its precinct.

I wake with the sun to find
A horizon line has made me blind.

Waiting as day, unfurling, fills,
And hills fade back into other hills,
I too could start again at naught
In the clear-sighted view
Beyond a lost train of thought.

DIPTYCH NATIVITY

I.

On Christmas Day the hoarfrost's sheen
Of silver, red, gold, and green,

Will play like light inside a prism,
Then scatter in a vapor-schism.

Briefly, tonight, the marrow bone
Of mystery, the whole, is known.

The congregants are swearing by it
Throughout the interlude of quiet

After midnight, when the bonds
Of harmonies rise up like fronds,

Branching out across the vault,
Until each sees the other's fault.

II.

A painting near the altar depicts
St. George, a soldier who's transfixed

His horse's dragonish reflection,
The foil of his divine affection,

Stabbing it earthward with his lance
Until there's nothing left to chance

But emptiness, which God is in
Like forgiveness for a sin.

A hinge away, a Sienese
Madonna stares, as if she sees

A guest approaching in the night.
She holds up her infant like a light.

THE BISHOP'S TOMB IN MONTEFIASCONE

Non est hic (He is not here).—Matthew 28:6

The priest who found the sign
It's here! It's here!! It's here!!!
Is here. He stayed so long
He caved to local gods
Of boiling eels in wine
And nodding off at synods.

Est! Est!! Est!!! His tomb
Is his flask, his wish is clear
In stone. His spirit's trip
To God became his body's.
Above the caryatids
Like fat men playing cards,

A palimpsest of frescoes
In patches on pocked walls
Resembles a fabled life
Or a half-remembered dream
That's neither true nor false
For being somewhere else.

Sometimes this world is fog
As thick as any curd.
What do a last-ditch prayer
And a marinated cleric
Have in common? The word
That answers them is here.

BALLADE OF TIMOTHY MURPHY

after Richard Wilbur

Who was the man who could recall
His Auden, Yeats, and de la Mare,
And liked to make his poems small
And chatty, with a talker's flair
For drafting quatrains by the pair,
In meters that are sprightly, trim,
And North Dakota debonair?
He was, inimitably, Tim.

What Yalie had such wherewithal
For song in words that he was heir
To Hardy with a Yankee drawl
And Frost served up with Catholic fare?
What dude made Anglo-Saxon blare
American, and out of dim
Old *Beowulf* wrote verse with hair?
That singing contradiction, Tim.

Who had the energy and gall
To foster hogs and laissez-faire,
And nearly drown in alcohol
And find a Light in his despair?
Whose love of hunting, men, and prayer
Had fiery Irish verve and vim
That time and troubles didn't wear?
Intrepid never tepid Tim.

But it's beside the point to air
This fit of rhyme recalling him,
Because his rhymes themselves declare
The man who authored them was Tim.

Murmuration After a Storm at Rush Hour

Termini Station, Rome

Off like a dream, our tired commute
      This evening starts as we walk under
            Squalls of starlings which dispute
                  Departing arguments that thunder

This evening starts, as we walk under
      Babbling streams of starling-pulses,
            Departing arguments that thunder
Extends in rolls, and then convulses

          Babbling streams of starling; pulses,
Billows, and spins, as heaving cloth
             Extends in rolls, and then convulses.
      Our longing sways in body's sloth,

Billows and spins as heaving cloth.
                    Who moves that rippling negligée?
          Our longing sways in body's sloth
              While starlings gown a bony tree.

          Who moves that rippling negligée
                    A phantom dancer swirls to fold,
              While starlings gown a bony tree
The clammy hands of hours hold?

                    A phantom dancer swirls to fold.
              Squalls of starlings which dispute
          The clammy hands of hours hold
Off like a dream our tired commute.

Maria Luisa Spaziani

SEVEN P.M.

The bottle shards, like scales atop the wall—
orange, lilac, ocher, blue of Chartres—
reflect the setting sun
on the lane at nightfall.

An elm tree overflows: arrows of whorls,
cackles, calls, tumult of wings' upheavals.

Flotsam of defunct cathedrals,
shimmering fragments, wall.

Estranged: Lines of an American Expat

Our smoldering has turned to smoke
That streaks the sky like contrails spread
Across the sea. Your fertile body
Gave me a life before I woke
To sleepwalk where my dreams had led,
Oblivious there'd been a rift.
Though distant, you still have your hooks
In me. Your plain talk has gone shoddy,
Your ruddy natural good looks
Are faded, yet your undertow
Still raises riptides in my blood.
Marking our continental drift
Apart, our fits of fire and flood
Are all goodbye and half hello.
My mother, my love, our past runs deep.
We don't know what is going wrong,
To whom or where we now belong,
As we turn and toss and turn in sleep.

Storm Watch in Upper Lazio

2020

The valley lies as if in wait—for what?
A gray processional of cluster clouds
Advances southward over silent crowds
Of anonymity. We feel the glut
Of discontent inside the gathering distance.
Masks inter our faces at our breath's insistence.

*

The *Pax Romana* broods a pregnant calm,
Agitated by the rhetoric
Of politicians "for the people" (*sic*).
At rush hour, talk shows detonate a bomb
Of blame that shudders down the motorway.
The ones who know the secret soon will have their day.

Friction billows high up in the ether,
Cumulus-cloudy, while the *populus*
Dissolves from all-for-one to them and us,
Till both sides vaporize their or and either.
Candidate-vandals, having seized the Quirinal's
Pomp, graffiti voting booths like walls of urinals.

*

Lightning bolts are jagging through the dark
Of a storm cloud. The cloud's about to burst!
Many are called, the last will be the first
To drown. Romulus sails his homemade ark
Along the Tiber, bearded, old, and vatic,
With pairs from every species, finally democratic.

THE TYRANT

Cain . . . built a city.—Genesis 4:17

The puddle of blood in the dirt
Beside Abel's carcass
Shivers. And a curse
Rises screeching from earth,
As if to flee the darkness.

His shuddering scuds by
On frozen wings. Nervous,
I look about me: nobody.
Just the familiar empty
Field, the failed harvest.

Here is the place I'll build,
Where I am the only guest.
When my brother and I reached the field,
I raised the rock and growled:
This is for being blessed.

UNREQUITED LIKE

I'll tell you, friends, a crazy nothing thing,
    If telling is for listening
To how warm air inside a mouth condenses:
I've shot my wad, my woof, my puff of life,
    As if to make the best of strife
By getting good at sitting on my fences,
       For unrequited like.

Yup, you (if there's a you to hear) heard right.
    Despite disparagement or spite
From who knows who, or so-called common sense
Regarding outcomes that are coming out,
    A lover's faith that lives with doubt
And doesn't wring the world for recompense
      Is what I want and like.

IV. Birds and the Hours

Melt with joy upon the dark.

—David Mason

SONG

The most delicious truth is flesh,
The secret of the everyday,
Where women are a walking wish
And kids come out to play.

The Trojan warriors hated Paris
Because he liked his love too much.
Within a knot of sheets and hair, his
Revenge had lost its touch.

I, living in a softer age,
Have always understood his plight,
Preferring musky skin to rage
And beauty to a fight.

GUIDO GUINIZZELLI

I want to give my lady honest praise

I want to give my lady honest praise,
And liken her to lily and to rose;
More radiant than Venus's dawn rays,
Whatever beauty heaven has, she shows.
I say she's like the meadows, April air,
All colors, primrose-yellow, poppy-red,
Gold, lapis, jewels—everything that's rare;
And even Love in her is better-bred.

As she walks by, all loveliness and grace,
She makes your knees bend with greeting—your pride
Collapses and you're instantly devout.
A man cannot get near her who is base.
And one more, greater virtue I'll confide:
In seeing her, all meanness is snuffed out.

Anima

Her skin marine, her fragrance haze,
Eyes buoys that mark the harbor.
Her length awash in waterways
While ruddering limbs ride the currents.
Her womb capacious, the ocean's loom.

She lives in bodies' salt recurrence,
The lit electrolytes and sonar lore
Below: queen of the drifting sanctum,
A lone blue whale whose purlieus are
The billowing domains of plankton.

SMITTEN

It was as if she'd taken a resin-soaked,
Turpentined, skull-bone cloth surrounded
By paint buckets all spattered and packed
With brushes and stirring sticks, landed
Haphazard in a cramped unventilated
Basement, like a magazine of shadows shunned;
Taken that rag of poison baited
With pine, the most combustible compound
The mad corporate chemists could invent
(And all the while her face rainbowed
Across her widening light's blue tint,
Became translucent, new, unflawed);
Taken it and with a match's kiss
Blown up the works—me, her, and it.

In a Renaissance Bishop's Garden

With swelling cupolas and cornucopias,
The hillside garden is a theme park for us
Still: an architectural thesaurus
Of body's dream of on-the-spot utopias.

Its fountains are a learned priest's creations,
As link by link they gurgle liquid chains
That coil into pools to sluice through veins
Of statues wet with spouts' ejaculations.

The sound of water: how describe it? Purl
And tinkle, lave and lap, lip-sync a song
Of shade in summer, when the light is long
And oyster-mind secretes a body-pearl.

The naiads in the water speak in tongues,
Baffling to anti-Babel gospel fire.
Their hefty haunches strain to push them higher
While tritons shinny down the angel-rungs.

A stone boy laughs in plashes from a grotto
As if he's overheard a sober motto.

CRISTINA CAMPO

LAST DANCE STEP

For last year's words belong to last years' language and next year's words await another voice. (T. S. Eliot)

The bright white gowns of summer fold again
as you descend on the meridian,
October, lovely, on nests.

The closing song is trembling in loggias,
where the sun was shadow, shadow sun,
with breathlessness at rest.

And while the lukewarm rose postpones departure,
the bitter berry drips already with the taste
of smiling farewells.

CRISTINA CAMPO

My love, today your name

My love, today your name
slipped from my lip
as from a foot the final step . . .

Now the water of life is sprinkled
and all the lengthy stairway
has to be started over.

I traded you, my love, for words.

Dark honey spreading your scent
inside diaphanous vases
beneath a thousand six hundred years of lava—

I'll recognize you by undying
silence.

SILVER LOVERS

If you and I were plates
Set neatly on a table,
We'd be such even mates
We'd never be unstable.

Or covers of a book
With a long tale between:
We'd miss each other's look
And what the look might mean.

Or, say, a door ajar
Aslant a strident hinge:
We'd wake to who we are
With every opening twinge.

Or else a pair of shoes
In tandem locomotion:
Which would be which, whose whose?
Our steps would be devotion.

As long parallel tracks
Converging in a field,
We wouldn't turn our backs
On what our differences yield.

At last, as lanky grasses,
Who could tell us apart
Once the mower passes,
Impartial in his art?

We know we're silver lovers,
Our tarnish is understood,
So let's crawl in the covers
And shine our silver good.

Birds and the Hours

I raise my window blind
To see if the morning air will change my mind.
The world outside is busy taking flight.
    My linden's loud with finches'
  Diminutively bold delight,
      Their game of inches.

I want to see the source but when I turn
To look at the branches' waving hands it's gone.

    A celebrated myth
Of a night bird depicts a sister with
A severed tongue, alone in the dark but free
      To right the daylight's wrong
  And nurse invisibility
        To turn to song.

At dawn her solo vanishes in choirs.
The day will scatter voices with the hours.

JUNIOR SOCCER

You'd think the ball was a germ, the kids
Exuberant antibodies swarming
To douse it with will, then finally
Punish it toward the orange witch-hats goal.

My friend's daughter doesn't want us to know
She's eager for us to watch her jostle
Her little body into the skirmish.
Her hair's an antenna for attention,

But she never turns, having learned to hide
Childish reliance on Mom's esteem.
She still can't grasp the rationale of rules
Or which of the brawling feet are on her team.

One boy, the coach's son, suddenly head-butts
The ball above a small astonished melee
Of teammates contending with each other,
The younger kids intent on getting only

Some piece of themselves to touch it,
Like tongues waiting to catch the first raindrop,
The older ones more focused, their faces
Braced: balanced surfaces of water.

The small girl who invited me here floats
To the sidelines, absentmindedly alone,
Staring into the trees behind the school,
Before she remembers again we're watching.

Moon Commute

What in this rocking and clacking,
This plummeting headlong into what
Mirrors a window backed by black
And the streetlights speeding back:
What does the traveler commute?

Can any of what he is or has
Come home? Oblivion beguiles
In sultry dulcet brass jazz
Purling in earbuds. For miles,
Kinda kinda black, he dozes.

The lives he's lived and lost appear
In shadows shuffling in haze
By water, people's features blurry,
Pearly in circle-light. And the days
Drift back inside a silver mirror.

NOTES

The Distance

Ce la faremo = "We'll get through this," "We can do it," etc.
afa = hot, muggy air

The Bishop's Tomb in Montefiascone

Est! Est!! Est!!! is an Italian white wine based in Montefiascone, a town in central Italy near where I live.
Wikipedia says of the story behind it: "The unusual
name of the wine region dates back to a 12th-century
tale of a German bishop traveling to the Vatican for a
meeting with the pope. The bishop sent a prelate ahead
of him to survey the villages along the route for the best
wines. The 'wine scout' had instructions to write 'Est'
(Latin for 'There is') on the door or on the wall of the
inns he visited when he was particularly impressed with
the quality of the wine they served so the bishop following on his trail would have known in advance where to
make a stop. At a Montefiascone inn, the prelate was
reportedly so overwhelmed with the local wine that he
wrote *Est! Est!! Est!!!* on the door."

MARIA LUISA SPAZIANI: Seven P.M.

Maria Luisa Spaziani (1924–2014) was a scholar and poet from Turin. She is also known from her association with the poet Eugenio Montale—she is the muse-figure "Volpe" ("Fox") he writes about in his collection *La bufera* (The Storm), published in 1956. This poem alludes to Montale's famous early poem "Meriggiare pallido e assorto [Repose at midday pallid and reflective]."

GUIDO GUINIZZELLI: *I want to give my lady honest praise*

Guido Guinizzelli (ca. 1225–76), from Bologna, was a highly influential love poet and father of the so-called *dolce stil novo* (sweet new style) that Dante named and made famous. This is a translation of Guinizzelli's sonnet *Io voglio del ver la mia donna laudare.*

CRISTINA CAMPO: Last Dance Step and *My love, today your name*

The writer, translator, and independent scholar Cristina Campo (1923–77) was a pseudonym of the Bolognese Vittoria Guerrini, who moved to Rome in 1955 and stayed there for the remainder of her life. These poems are from her 1956 collection *Passo d'addio,* of which "Last Dance Step" is the title poem.

ACKNOWLEDGMENTS

My grateful acknowledgments go to the editors of the following online and print publications, in which these poems first appeared, sometimes in earlier versions: *Alabama Literary Review, Amethyst Review, The Atlantic, Hudson Review, Light Quarterly, Literary Review, Modern Age, New Criterion, New Verse News, New York Sun, Plough, Prairie Schooner, Pulsebeat Poetry Journal, Temenos Academy Review, THINK, Trinity House Review, Unsplendid, Western Humanities Review, Wine Cellar Press.* A few of the poems were previously collected, in earlier versions, in my chapbook *Death of a Dissembler* (White Violet Press, 2014); my thanks to Karen Kelsay for permission to reprint them.

"Seven P.M.," by Maria Luisa Spaziani, is translated from her poem originally called "Le sette di sera," taken from *Geometria del disordine* (Milan, 1981) and published with permission from Mondadori Libri S.p.A.

Cristina Campo's poems "Last Dance Step" ("Passo d'addio") and *My love, today your name* (*Amore, oggi il tuo nome*) are translated and published with permission of Adelphi Edizioni, from the volume Cristina Campo, *La tigre assenza* (Milan, 1991), edited by Margherita Pieracci Harwell.

I am grateful to the poets on Eratosphere, and A. M. Juster, Siham Karami, Lisa McCabe, Giulia Sorrentino, and especially Daphne Lull, to whom this book is dedicated, for feedback and encouragement.

ABOUT THE AUTHOR

ANDREW FRISARDI is a writer, translator, critic, and editor from Boston who lives in the Lazio region of Italy. His previous books of poetry are the full-length collection *The Harvest and the Lamp* (Franciscan UP, 2020) and a chapbook, *Death of a Dissembler* (White Violet Press, 2014). He has also authored two books of literary essays: *Ancient Salt: Essays on Poets, Poetry, and the Modern World* (Resource Publications, 2022) and *Love's Scribe: Reading Dante in the Book of Creation* (Angelico Press, 2020). Frisardi's dual-language critical edition of Dante's *Convivio* was published by Cambridge University Press in 2018, and his annotated translation of Dante's *Vita nova* was published by Northwestern University Press in 2012; and he has also published translations of the dialect poet Franco Loi (Counterpath, 2008) and the modernist poet Giuseppe Ungaretti (Farrar, Straus & Giroux, 2004). His poems and translations have been published in *The Atlantic, Hudson Review, New Criterion, New Republic,* the *New Yorker, THINK,* and many other journals in print and online. His work has been awarded with a Guggenheim Fellowship, a Hawthornden Literary Fellowship, and the Raiziss / de Palchi Translation Award from the Academy of American Poets.

Made in the USA
Middletown, DE
23 September 2023

39038340R00056